MW01028492

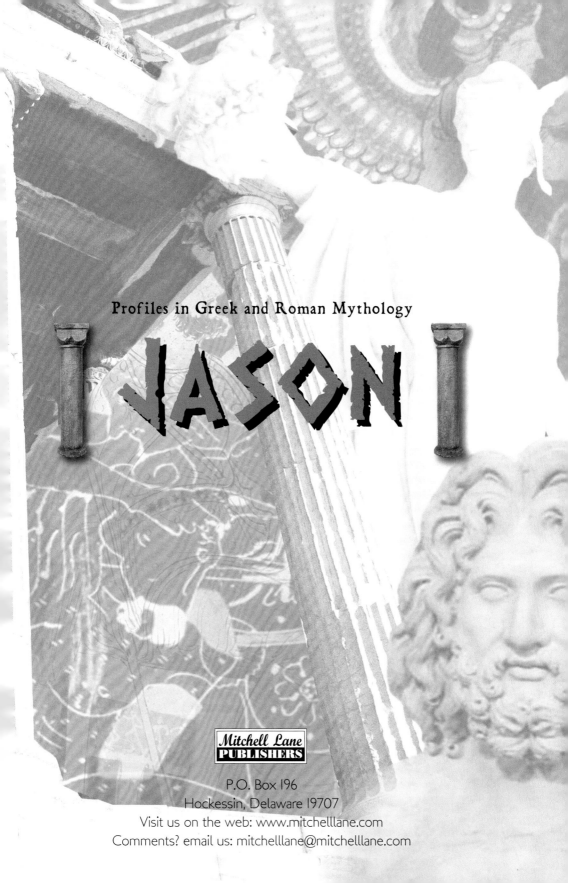

Profiles in Greek and Roman Mythology

JASON

Mitchell Lane
PUBLISHERS

P.O. Box 196
Hockessin, Delaware 19707
Visit us on the web: www.mitchelllane.com
Comments? email us: mitchelllane@mitchelllane.com

PROFILES IN GREEK AND ROMAN MYTHOLOGY

Titles in the Series

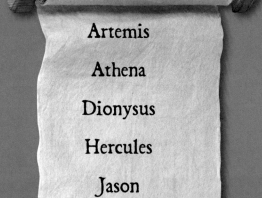

Profiles in Greek and Roman Mythology

JASON

Jim Whiting

Mitchell Lane
PUBLISHERS

P.O. Box 196
Hockessin, Delaware 19707
Visit us on the web: www.mitchelllane.com
Comments? email us: mitchelllane@mitchelllane.com

Mitchell Lane
PUBLISHERS

Printing   1   2   3   4   5   6   7   8   9

Library of Congress Cataloging-in-Publication Data
Whiting, Jim, 1943-

    Jason / by Jim Whiting.

        p. cm. — (Profiles in Greek and Roman mythology)
      Includes bibliographical references and index.
      ISBN 978-1-58415-552-2 (library bound)
      1. Jason (Greek mythology) — Juvenile literature. 1. Title.
      BL820.A8W45 2007
      398.2'0983801 — dc22

                                     2007000771

ABOUT THE AUTHOR: Jim Whiting has been a remarkably versatile and accomplished journalist, writer, editor, and photographer for more than 30 years. He has made seven trips to Greece, during which time he immersed himself in the country's fabulous history and culture. A voracious reader since early childhood, Mr. Whiting has written and edited more than 250 nonfiction children's books on a wide range of topics. He lives in Washington state with his wife and two teenage sons.

PHOTO CREDITS: p. 6—Jonathan Scott; pp. 11, 16, 38—Barbara Marvis; p. 17—Manchester City Art Gallery

AUTHOR'S NOTE: The legend of Jason has numerous variations. This version follows *The Argonautika: The Story of Jason and the Quest for the Golden Fleece* by Apollonius of Rhodes, generally considered the most complete version of the myth. The other primary source is *Medea* by the Greek playwright Euripides. Portions of this story have been retold using dialogue as an aid to readability. The dialogue is based on the author's extensive research and approximates what might have occurred at the time.

    To reflect current usage, we have chosen to use the secular era designations BCE ("before the common era") and CE ("of the common era") instead of the traditional designations BC ("before Christ") and AD (*anno Domini,* "in the year of the Lord").

PLB

TABLE OF CONTENTS

Profiles in Greek and Roman Mythology

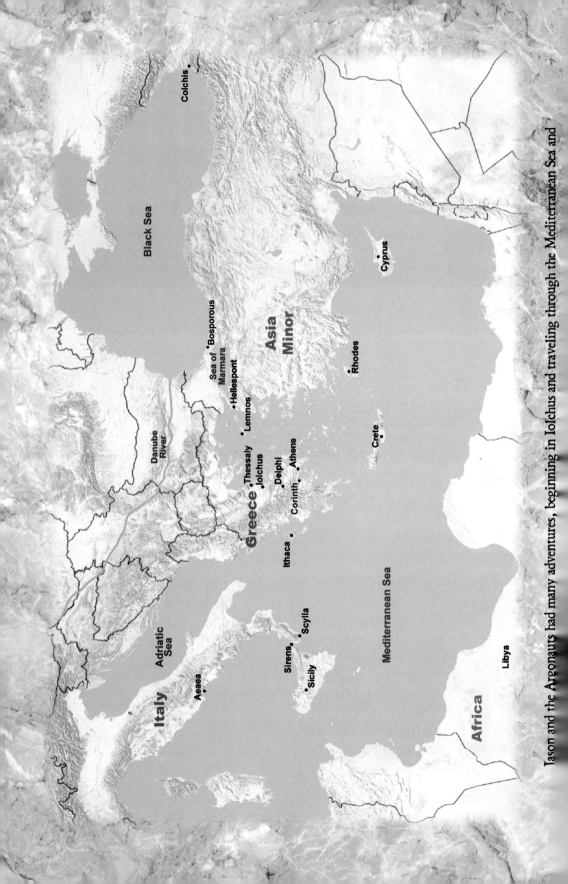

Jason and the Argonauts had many adventures, beginning in Iolchus and traveling through the Mediterranean Sea and

CHAPTER 1

A Monstrous Crime

It is one of the most frightening of all the Greek myths. At the climax of the play *Medea* (mee-DEE-uh), by ancient Greek playwright Euripides (yuh-RIP-uh-deez), the audience hears a bloodcurdling shriek from a young boy who is offstage. Then he screams hysterically:

> O help us, in God's name, for now we need your help.
> Now, now we are close to it. We are trapped by the sword.[1]

Moments later, both the boy and his brother are dead. They have been murdered, which is awful enough. What is even more horrible is the identity of the murderer. Her name is Medea, and she is their mother.

When a mother kills her children today, it evokes outrage and makes national news. It is easy to imagine the shock and horror that the audience must have felt. They had just listened to Medea say exactly what she was going to do. She was striking at what is one of the most sacred bonds among humans: the relationship between a mother and her children. Killing her sons certainly wasn't easy for her. She told herself to do the foul deed quickly, to make her heart of steel. Above all, she had to forget how sweet the children were and the fact that she was their mother. If she couldn't do that, she added, she would be a coward.

Moments later she rushed into her house, carrying a sword. Typical of Greek theater, the audience didn't actually witness the crime. As they heard the children's screams of agony, their imaginations could easily fill in the details.

The children's father, Jason, is angry and appalled by what Medea has just done. He says to her:

> You hateful thing, you woman most utterly loathed
> By the gods and me and by all the race of mankind,
> You who have had the heart to raise a sword against
> Your children, you, their mother, and left me childless—
> You have done this, and do you still look at the sun
> And at the earth, after these most fearful doings?[2]

Today we are accustomed to murderous mothers being brought to justice. Sometimes they are sent to prison for their crime. Sometimes they are deemed so mentally disturbed that they undergo years of treatment. The important thing is that they don't get away with what they have done. Jason also expects Medea to pay for her actions:

> For she will have to hide herself beneath the earth,
> Or raise herself on wings into the height of air,
> If she wishes to escape the royal vengeance.[3]

Ready to take matters into his own hands, Jason issues orders to the people surrounding him:

> Quick as you can unlock the doors, men, and undo
> The fastenings and let me see this double evil,
> My children dead and her—Oh her I will repay.[4]

He is too late. Carrying the limp bodies of the two children, she appears on top of the house in a chariot drawn by dragons. She mocks Jason: "You will never touch me with your hand."[5]

Then she tells him that she is going to escape to the city of Athens, where the citizens will actually welcome her. In fact, she will found a race of people who will eventually come back to cause the Greeks a great deal of grief.

This scene provides a sad and violent ending to one of the most famous Greek myths: Jason and the Argonauts (AR-goh-nots). The story of Jason and the men who sailed with him is one of the very first epic myths in human history. Many scholars believe that it also contains the first love story.

It is significant for yet another reason. As historian and adventurer Tim Severin notes, "The actual ship that carried the heroes, the immortal *Argo*, is the first vessel in recorded history to bear a name. To a seaman, this has a powerful appeal: for the first time a boat is something more than an inanimate floating object, an anonymous vehicle. *Argo* is a named, identifiable boat which has a character of her own. In the ancient telling of the story *Argo* could speak with a human voice, and at crucial moments state her own opinions."[6]

The events in the myth supposedly take place during the thirteenth century BCE. No one knows when the first version of the story was told. Many scholars believe that it began in the tenth or ninth century BCE, though an earlier date is possible.

"This area of Thessaly is now known to have been a center of the development of early epic poetry in the centuries before Homer," notes archaeologist Michael Wood. "Indeed it was in palaces like Iolkos [Iolchus] in the late Bronze Age that Greek bards first advanced from heroic songs or praise poems of a few hundred lines to extended epics of several thousand [lines], telling stories of many episodes."[7]

The story of the Argonauts was already well known by the time of the great Greek poet Homer, who is usually dated in the eighth century BCE. He mentions *Argo* in his epic poem the *Odyssey*: "The *Argo*, sung by the world."[8]

Additional versions of the story appeared over the next few centuries. Euripides probably wrote his *Medea* in the late fifth century BCE. The "definitive version"—the one that is best known today—arose during the following century. Called *The Argonautika*

(ar-goh-NAW-tih-kuh), it was written by Apollonius (aa-paa-LOH-nee-us) of Rhodes. (Rhodes, Apollonius' birthplace, is one of the largest Greek islands.)

Like all the other variants—and like many other Greek myths—Apollonius' story rests on a somewhat complicated series of stormy family relationships. Jason's father Aeson (EE-son) was the rightful king of a region known as Thessaly, but his half brother Pelias (PEE-lee-us) took control instead. To be sure that he would remain king, Pelias threw Aeson into prison and killed several of their relatives.

Aeson's wife, Polymele (pah-luh-MEE-lee), gave birth to a son, Jason. "Pelias would have destroyed the child without mercy, had not Polymele summoned her kinswomen to weep over him, as though he were still-born, and then smuggled him out of the city,"[9] points out classical scholar Robert Graves. Safely away from Pelias, Jason lived with a centaur (SEN-tar) named Cheiron (KY-rohn), who was noted for his general wisdom and knowledge of medicine.

When he grew up, Jason decided to return to the capital of Thessaly, Iolchus (eye-OL-kus), to restore his father to his rightful position. He approached the city during a festival to Poseidon (poh-SY-dun), the god of the sea. He came to a stream that was at flood stage. An old woman sat beside it, dejected because she wasn't strong enough to cross by herself and everyone she had asked for help ignored her. Jason said he would be glad to carry her. He hoisted her onto his back, then began crossing the stream. As he struggled with the extra weight, one of his sandals fell off and the current carried it away. He set the woman down on the other side and continued on his journey.

The old woman was actually Hera (HAYR-uh), one of the twelve gods and goddesses of Greece. She was also the wife of Zeus (ZOOS), the chief god. She didn't like Pelias because she didn't feel that he paid enough honor to her. As a result, she wanted to help Jason.

Years earlier, while Jason was still on his mountain retreat with Cheiron, Pelias had heard a prophecy: A man with one sandal would be dangerous to him. When he now saw Jason staggering in with just one sandal, he realized that his enemy had finally arrived.

He wanted to get rid of Jason, but he couldn't just kill him outright. He told Jason that he would restore his father Aeson to the throne if Jason completed a quest for him. Pelias asked Jason what the most difficult quest would be.

Mount Olympus, in northern Greece, was believed to be the home of the Greek gods and goddesses. It is more than 9,000 feet high.

To get the golden fleece, Jason replied.

Both Jason and Pelias would have been very familiar with the story of the golden fleece. It involved two of Jason's cousins, Phrixus (FRIK-sus) and Helle (HEH-lee), the children of Nephele (NEF-uh-lee) and King Athamas (ATH-uh-mas), who ruled the important town of Orchomenus (or-KUH-meh-nus). Athamas eventually decided that he wanted another wife. He married Ino (EYE-noh), and they had two sons. She wanted them to succeed Athamas as ruler when he died, but Phrixus was older than her children and therefore ahead of them in the line of succession.

Ino plotted to get rid of Phrixus. She treated the city's seed grain so that it wouldn't grow very well. The harvest that year was so poor, the people of Orchomenus were afraid they might starve. In that era, people would ask the Oracle at Delphi (DEL-fy) for predictions and advice in dealing with difficult situations.

No one knows what the oracle really said when the representatives from Orchomenus came to consult. Ino bribed them to tell Athamas a lie when they returned: The only way to restore the fertility of the land was for Athamas to sacrifice his son Phrixus. Athamas was appalled, but he felt he had no choice. He was about to cut Phrixus' throat when a golden ram sent down from Mount Olympus (the home of the gods) suddenly appeared.

Phrixus climbed on its back. Helle joined him because she was afraid she would be murdered if she stayed behind. The ram rose into the air and flew east, toward the city of Colchis (KOHL-kis). Located at the eastern shore of the Black Sea, Colchis was where the sun god Helios (HEE-lee-ohs) kept his horses.

Helle soon grew tired, lost her grip, and fell into the sea below. The spot where she fell is a narrow strait called the Hellespont (HEH-luh-spont). Located in modern-day Turkey and now known as the Dardanelles, it is part of the dividing line between Europe and Asia.

The ram continued on to Colchis. The ruler, king Aeëtes (ee-EE-teez), welcomed Phrixus. According to the ram's own instructions, Phrixus sacrificed it as an offering to Zeus. Then he removed its golden woolen hide and hung it over a thick branch in a sacred grove, where it had remained ever since.

Pelias knew that it would require a long, difficult, and dangerous voyage just to get to Colchis. Even if Jason somehow managed to complete the trip, there were other obstacles to obtaining the fleece. A dragon that never slept guarded it. King Aeëtes didn't want to let it go and would probably try to kill anyone who made the effort to take it. Pelias confidently assumed, therefore, that sending Jason on this quest would be a good way of getting rid of him—permanently.

Homer's *Odyssey*

The Cyclops Polyphemus

Homer composed two long epics about the Trojan War. One, *Iliad*, describes the events of the war during an especially crucial stage. The other, *Odyssey*, details the ten-year adventures of the Greek hero Odysseus (known as Ulysses to the Romans) as he and his men try to sail home to his native island of Ithaca after the war.

Early in this homeward journey, a giant Cyclops named Polyphemus (pah-lih-FEE-mus) captures him and his men and begins eating them. In desperation, Odysseus blinds him and makes his escape with his remaining men.

Unfortunately for Odysseus, Polyphemus is the son of the sea god Poseidon. Poseidon is angry with Odysseus and creates all sorts of difficulties for his voyage home. Odysseus has to endure attacks by monsters, shipwrecks, periods of captivity, his men getting into trouble, and much more. The other gods try to help out, but they can't run the risk of making Poseidon angry. Finally, alone of all the men from Ithaca who set out for the Trojan War, Odysseus is washed up on the shores of his native island.

His struggles don't end when he arrives home. In his absence, dozens of men have put pressure on his wife, Penelope, to marry them. They insist that Odysseus is dead and that she is now a widow. Penelope, however, remains faithful. Odysseus disguises himself as a beggar while he figures out what to do. Then, aided by his son Telemachus (tuh-LEH-muh-kus), who has also remained faithful to his father's memory, he tricks the men who have tried to marry Penelope and slays them all. Odysseus and Penelope are reunited.

Scholars aren't sure when Homer composed the *Odyssey*. The best estimate is sometime around the eighth or ninth century BCE. Along with the *Iliad*, the *Odyssey* is one of the best known literary works of all time. Today, the word *odyssey* means "a long and difficult journey."

An artist's conception of the *Argo*, the ship used by Jason and the Argonauts. When the vessel was under maximum power, the sail was up and all the men were rowing. The steering oar is located on the side near the rear of the ship.

JASON

CHAPTER 2

The *Argo* Sets Out

Jason didn't see the quest in the same way as Pelias. To him, it would be a great adventure, because no one except Phrixus had traveled so far to the east.

Jason hired a man named Argus to build the ship, which turned out to be the largest vessel that had ever been built up to that time. There was room for fifty men (twenty-five on each side) to row it. It also had a mast and sail, so the men could rest if the wind came up. It even had a talking timber, which would offer Jason advice at several important points in the story.

The ship's name was *Argo,* and the heroes who clambered on board were called Argonauts ("sailors of Argo"). *Argonaut* is similar to our modern word *astronaut,* which means "star sailor."

Jason put out a call for young men to go with him. Nearly all of the famous legendary Greek heroes answered, including Hercules (HER-kyoo-leez), Theseus (THEE-see-us), the Gemini twins Castor and Polydeuces (pah-lih-DOO-seez), Orpheus (OR-fee-us), and dozens more. "The crew of the *Argo* included the flower of Greece, descendants of gods and ancestors of Greek nobles,"[1] observe scholars Mark Morford and Robert Lenardon. There is, however, no definitive crew roster. "Lists of the Argonauts vary, since the Greeks of later ages were eager to claim an Argonaut for an ancestor,"[2] Morford and Lenardon add.

The Argonauts' first stop was at the island of Lemnos, where there were no men. At some point, the women who lived on Lemnos had offended Aphrodite (aa-froh-DY-tee), the goddess of love and beauty. In retaliation, she made them smell awful. Because they stank, their husbands began sleeping with their slave women instead. The wives

The Argonauts' first stop was at the island of Lemnos. At the time of their visit, the island was populated entirely by women.

killed the men and all the children they had had with these slave women.

The Lemnian women were very excited when the Argonauts arrived because it had been a long time since they had seen any men. Their leader was Hypsipyle (hip-SIH-puh-lee), the daughter of the former king. She wanted Jason to stay on Lemnos and become the island's new king. The other women invited the Argonauts into their homes and slept with them. They had a number of male children, which helped to repopulate the island.

Many of the men were having a good time and wanted to stay on Lemnos. When Hercules reminded them that this was just a place to stop briefly to rest before proceeding on their quest, the men went back to the *Argo* and left the island.

Soon they entered the Hellespont and proceeded into what is today known as the Sea of Marmara (MAR-muh-ruh). On the south coast, they stayed briefly at the land of the Doliones (doh-lee-OH-neez). Led by King Cyzicus (SIH-zuh-kus), the Doliones warmly greeted the travelers. The Argonauts left the next day, but a storm blew them back to the island that night. In the darkness, the Doliones didn't recognize the men whom they just had treated as welcome guests. They thought the men were invaders. A battle broke out, and many Doliones were killed. Then everyone realized the tragic mistake. The Argonauts pushed on grimly.

To break up the monotony of the journey, the men held a rowing contest. Hercules pulled so hard that he broke his oar. The *Argo* had to come ashore so that he could make a new one. His friend Hylas (HY-las) wandered into the forest. A water nymph saw Hylas, who was very handsome. She fell in love with him and drew him down into a freshwater spring. When Hercules realized that Hylas had disappeared, he went to look for him. Though he went deeper and deeper into the forest, he couldn't find his friend.

In the meantime, a fresh breeze blew up. Jason wanted to take advantage of it and continue the journey. Reluctantly he made the decision to leave Hercules behind. It may have been just as well. Hercules was in the midst of his Twelve Labors. It was time for him to go back home and finish them.

English painter John William Waterhouse shows the attraction between Hercules' handsome friend Hylas and a water nymph. She and her friends took him deep into this spring.

The next adventure involved a fierce king named Amycus (AA-muh-kus), a heavyset man of great strength who forced every traveler passing through his kingdom to box with him. He had never lost a match and had killed several men. In spite of Amycus' reputation, Polydeuces decided he would fight. He was the exact opposite physically—a slender young man who was very quick on his feet.

Amycus began the bout by rushing straight at Polydeuces, swinging his fists wildly. Polydeuces simply stepped out of the way. Then the two men traded blows for a long time. Polydeuces used his agility to step away from the harder jabs.

Finally Amycus tried to land an especially hard blow. Polydeuces took it on his shoulder, then pivoted and landed his fist just behind Amycus' ear. It cracked the skull bones and the king fell dead.

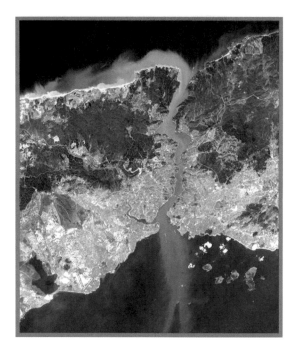

A satellite image of the Bosporus, the narrow strait that connects the Black Sea with the Sea of Marmara. Its strong currents have always made its passage treacherous.

Soon the Argonauts entered the Bosporus (BOS-peh-rus), another narrow body of water that also separates Europe from Asia and leads into the Black Sea. Even today, it is an area of deadly currents. As Tim Severin notes, the Bosporus "presented a vast disturbed mass of water spewing south . . . at 3–4 knots . . . broken into white caps and short maverick waves by the wind."[3]

Not everyone is willing to dare the passage. "Before the days of motor power, the normal practice for boats going upstream [into the Black Sea] was to wait until one of the rare southerly winds arose, which at least slowed the current and, if strong enough, could be used under sail,"[4] Severin explains. An alternative was to go ashore, fasten lines to the boat, and pull it. But the Argonauts were in hostile territory, at risk of being attacked if they landed. That left just one alternative: muscle power.

Even muscle power was often not enough. The currents could turn the *Argo* broadside to the waves and swamp it. The helmsman, Tiphys (TY-fis), had to use all of his considerable talent to keep the boat from being overturned.

As they slowly made their way up the Bosporus, they encountered a seer named Phineus (FIH-nee-us), who had a reputation for making accurate prophecies. At one point, he had revealed more than the gods wanted people to know, so Zeus punished him by striking him blind. That wasn't the only punishment. Phin-

Zetes and Calais protect Phineus from the Harpies, who have kept him from eating. The Harpies were a combination of women and birds.

eus was nearly starving to death because hideous birdlike monsters called Harpies would descend anytime that someone brought food to him. They would steal nearly all of it, and put a horrible smell over what little was left behind. No one—not even someone on the verge of starvation—could stand to eat it.

The Argonauts offered to help. Two of the heroes, Zetes (ZEE-teez) and Calais (kah-LAY-us), gave food to Phineus and stood guard. As soon as the Harpies appeared, they chased them away. The heroes wanted to kill them, but Iris, a minor god, told them not to. She promised that the Harpies would never bother Phineus again.

In return, Phineus gave the Argonauts some very useful advice. The major obstacle still lay ahead. Called the Symplegades (sim-

PLEE-gah-dez), it was a pair of huge rocks that continually smashed into each other. No ship could get between them and emerge into the Black Sea before getting crushed.

To make it, Phineus instructed, the Argonauts should release a dove. If it flew through the rocks, it would be safe for the men to follow. If it couldn't make it, then they shouldn't try either.

The dove barely eked its way past the rocks, losing a tail feather or two to the clashing rocks. The Argonauts decided to try their luck. At first they couldn't make any headway. The current was against them and large waves threatened to swamp the boat. The rocks continued to shudder as if they were about to crash together. If that happened, everyone would be lost. They would need the help of the gods. Then, as Apollonius relates:

> Athena [uh-THEE-nuh], left hand jammed against a massive
> Rock, with her right thrust *Argo* through and onward,
> And the vessel sped, airborne, like a swift-winged arrow;
> yet still the Rocks, as they violently met, sheared off the tip
> of her curving [stern], with its ornament.[5]

The Argonauts had done it! Long before, the gods had decreed that the immense rocks would be fixed in place the first time men traveled successfully between them. From that time on, sailors could proceed by the Symplegades without the fear of being crushed.

After passing through the Symplegades, the Argonauts were in the Black Sea. The hard part of the trip was over. The even harder part was about to begin.

The Labors of Hercules

Hercules, whose father was Zeus, had a reputation of being the strongest man on earth. He showed his strength when he was just an infant by strangling two huge poisonous snakes. Sometimes he used his gift unwisely. In a fit of madness, he murdered his wife and children. As punishment, he was forced to serve his cousin Eurystheus (yuh-RIS-thee-us), the king of Mycenae (my-SEE-nee), who ordered Hercules to do a series of very difficult and dangerous tasks, or labors, for him. Eurystheus hated his cousin and hoped that he would be killed while performing the labors.

Hercules attacks the Hydra, a many-headed monster, in one of his twelve labors.

The first labor involved killing the Nemean Lion, a ferocious beast with a skin that couldn't be penetrated by a spear or arrow. Hercules fought it barehanded and strangled it. Afterward he wore the lion's skin, which made him even stronger.

Then he had to kill the Hydra, a beast with many heads. Every time one of the heads was cut off, two more would replace it. Hercules finally figured out that if he put a torch to the stump right after he cut it off, new heads couldn't grow back. That was the end of the Hydra.

After two more labors, he set off with the Argonauts. When he returned, he resumed his task. The labors became more and more difficult. He had to travel farther and farther from home to complete them. In the last one, he had to descend into the Underworld and bring back Cerberus (SIR-bur-us), the three-headed dog that guarded the entrance. Once again, he could only use his bare hands. As was the case with the other eleven labors, he was successful.

After completing the labors, he had many other adventures. In the final one, he died when he put on a garment that had been coated with poison. He became immortal and was welcomed into Mount Olympus with the Greek gods and goddesses.

Seventeenth-century Flemish painter Erasmus Quillen shows Jason carrying the golden fleece past the statue of Ares, the god of war. Jason's confident stride shows that he is proud of his accomplishment.

JASON

CHAPTER 3

The Golden Fleece

Though the Argonauts had several adventures as they made their way east along the coast of modern-day Turkey, they weren't as dangerous or as complicated as the ones they had previously encountered. There probably was a good reason for this relative ease. As Michael Wood points out, "Sailing on the [Black Sea] itself is 'neither difficult nor dangerous,' as the 1850s *Black Sea Pilot* says reassuringly . . . once you are through the rocks and turn eastwards towards the rising sun, the circular current of the sea bears you along the Turkish coast."[1]

The Argonauts narrowly escaped a pitched battle with the Amazons, a race of fierce women. It probably would have cost a few of them their lives. The Amazons were expert warriors.

An important stop was at the island of Ares, where they rescued four castaways. These were the four sons of Phrixus, who had married Aeëtes' daughter Chalciope (kal-KYE-oh-pee). The sons agreed to help Jason with Aeëtes. They explained to Jason that Aeëtes was a strong king who was very suspicious of strangers. As we might say today, he was the kind of man who would "shoot first and ask questions later."

Even if the Argonauts weren't killed right away, Phrixus' sons explained, Aeëtes probably wouldn't want to give up the golden fleece. It wouldn't be possible to take it by force, because the king's army was too large and too powerful. Besides, they added, it was guarded by a fearsome dragon that never slept.

Aware of the dangers they might encounter, the Argonauts waited until nightfall to cover the final few miles to Colchis. As Tim Severin

notes, "They were like burglars reconnoitering a well-protected mansion."[2]

Argus, one of Phrixus' sons, took over the steering. He guided them up the Phasis River, which lay next to the city. They decided to spend the night hidden deep among some reeds. They knew it could be dangerous if Aeëtes discovered them by accident. He didn't like intruders.

While the Argonauts slept, the goddesses Hera and Athena decided they wanted to help Jason. At first they were stumped as to how, then they figured out what to do. They asked Aphrodite, the goddess of love and beauty, to cause Medea, the daughter of King Aeëtes, to fall in love with Jason.

As soon as the heroes entered the king's palace, Eros, the son of Aphrodite, launched a love arrow at Medea. She took one look at Jason and became thoroughly smitten with her new guest.

Though Aeëtes was clearly unhappy to see his new visitors, the laws of hospitality required him to organize a banquet for them. According to those laws, it was necessary to treat guests—no matter how unexpected or unwelcome—with courtesy and safekeeping. Nevertheless, he made it clear that he wanted the Argonauts to leave—the sooner the better.

Jason replied that they didn't intend any harm to the kingdom. All they wanted was the golden fleece.

Aeëtes thought for a moment, then told Jason he could have the golden fleece—if he could pass four tests. First he had to capture two wild, fire-breathing bulls and yoke them to a plow. Second, he had to use them to plow a large field. Third, he had to plant dragon's teeth in the furrows he had just plowed. These teeth would quickly emerge as fierce, heavily armed warriors. Jason's fourth and final test was to kill all these warriors by himself.

Aeëtes was pleased with himself. Like Pelias, he was convinced that Jason couldn't possibly pass these tests. He would almost certainly die trying.

English artist Evelyn De Morgan painted Medea in 1889.
The Jason myth is featured in many artworks.

Jason was depressed because the tasks seemed beyond the ability of one man alone. In reality, it was. Argus suggested that Jason try to get help from Medea. Because she was a priestess, she would know some magic that could prove helpful. At this point, Jason didn't know that she had already fallen in love with him.

At dawn, Medea went to the shrine of Hecate (HEH-kah-tee), the goddess she served. Already she had decided to help Jason, even though this help would come at a heavy personal price. She had to turn her back on her own father.

At Argus' urging, Jason went to see Medea. As soon as he saw her, he realized that he was in love with her and promised to marry her.

Medea gave him a magic lotion that would protect him from the fire-breathing bulls, but it wouldn't help him when all the armed men sprang up. The men wouldn't be a problem, she explained, because she had also figured out a way of dealing with them.

The ordeal began the next morning when the bulls rushed out at him,

> exhaling
> Quick blasts of flame, roared, and a murderous fireball
> Engulfed Jason, hit him like lightning,
> but the girl's drugs saved him.[3]

He grabbed one bull by the horn and threw it to the ground. He tripped the other one, which stumbled and fell. Quickly discarding his shield so that he would have both hands free, he yoked the two oxen to his plow. At first they didn't want to move. He jabbed them gently with his spear and they slowly moved forward. With each stride they broke a yard or so of the hard-packed soil.

Jason dropped dragon's teeth into the furrows as he went along. He kept glancing back nervously. He wanted to be sure that the soldiers didn't spring from the ground before he was ready.

It took him most of the day to plow four acres. He unyoked the two bulls and they ran away. He was just in time. The soldiers were beginning to spring up from the ground. If they had all attacked him at once, they probably would have killed him. But they didn't.

At Medea's suggestion, Jason picked up a large stone and threw it into the midst of all the soldiers. Then he hid. The soldiers all thought that one of them had thrown the boulder at the others. They began attacking one another, hacking and killing. Almost all of them died during this fight, and Jason was able to kill the few who were left.

As night fell, King Aeëtes threw a great banquet for everyone. He honored Jason for achieving four seemingly impossible tasks and assured him that the following day he would receive the golden fleece. Jason and the Argonauts went back to the ship to sleep.

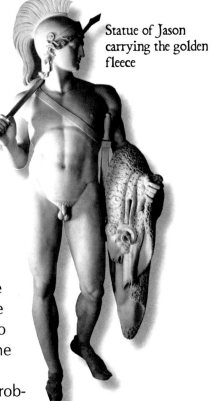

Statue of Jason carrying the golden fleece

King Aeëtes wasn't interested in sleeping. He didn't want to give Jason the golden fleece. The king tried to figure out how he would get rid of Jason—preferably by killing him.

Knowing her father's intention, Medea hurried down to where the ship was tied. She awakened the sleeping Argonauts and urged them to row to the sacred grove where the golden fleece was kept.

Even then Jason had to face a problem. The giant serpent that never slept

Though most versions of the myth state that Medea sprinkled magic dust on the eyes of the dragon to make it go to sleep, a few maintain that Jason was responsible. Italian artist Salvator Rosa, who flourished in the seventeenth century, takes this viewpoint.

guarded the fleece. Once again Medea came to Jason's aid. She looked at the serpent and began singing a mysterious melody that made it fall asleep. She kept singing and sprinkling magic dust on its eyes so that it would remain unconscious. With the serpent out of the way, Jason tugged the golden fleece down from its branch.

The two of them dashed back to the *Argo*. They hopped aboard and sailed down the river, aided by the favorable wind that Hera sent them. It appeared that Jason had succeeded in his quest. He had captured the golden fleece.

Amazons

The Amazons were a race of warriors who were all women. Some scholars believe that their name comes from two Greek roots: *a* (which means "without") and *mazos* (which means "breast"). Since ancient Greek archers drew their bowstrings back to their chest, a woman's right breast would get in the way. Therefore the Amazons would have their right breast removed when they were still very young.

Scholars Michael Grant and John Hazel offer a less gruesome explanation. "They did not make bread (*maza*, 'barley'), since they lived by hunting."[4] It could also mean "those who are not breast-fed."[5]

The Greeks in that era believed in male superiority. Because a race of warrior women would have been opposed to that belief, the Amazons' homeland was usually considered as being someplace very far away. One popular choice for the site was along the coast of the Black Sea in modern-day Turkey. That was at the fringe of the Greeks' known world.

The Amazons were regarded as excellent warriors, a close match to the Greeks. In addition to bows and arrows, they used swords, spears, and battleaxes. Normally they fought on horseback. Their queen was Hippolyte (hih-PAH-luh-tee), whose name means the "woman who lets the horses loose."

Metal artisan work showing the heavily armored Amazons

There are two theories about how the Amazons managed to have children. According to one, they would visit a neighboring kingdom once a year and spend a few days with the men there. When the children were born, little girls would be welcomed. Their mothers would raise them and teach them hunting and fighting. Boy babies that resulted from these unions were either killed on the spot or sent back to live with their fathers.

The other theory says that their society had both men and women. The men would be crippled not long after they were born. That way they could never present a threat to the women who controlled the society. These men would perform the tasks that women normally did in more traditional Greek societies: cooking, cleaning, taking care of children. The Amazons also acquired male captives in battle.

According to one version of the myth, Medea's brother Apsyrtus (reaching for his sister) accompanied Jason and Medea when they left Colchis. King Aeëtes personally led the pursuit. To slow him down, Medea killed Apsyrtus, cut his body into little pieces, and one by one threw them into the sea. Aeëtes had to stop and pick up each piece so that he could give his son a proper burial. These delays allowed Jason and Medea to make their escape.

JASON

CHAPTER 4

Homeward Bound

Up to this point, Apollonius' *Argonautika* and the other sources that relate the voyage of the Argonauts are very similar. This similarity ends as soon as Jason pushes off from Colchis and heads home.

"There are several different versions of the return of the *Argo*, which reflect different stages of Greek geographical knowledge," notes Michael Wood. "These versions cannot be reconciled, nor do the ancient authorities attempt to do so."[1]

While at least one source says that Medea's brother Apsyrtus (ap-SIR-tus) left Colchis with Jason and Medea, most others say Apsyrtus pursued them. King Aeëtes, who wasn't going to let the Argonauts go, ordered Apsyrtus to take a large force of men and set off in hot pursuit.

According to Apollonius, the Argonauts decided not to go back the same way they came, along the coast of Turkey. They thought it would be easier to escape if they headed for the mouth of the modern-day Danube River. According to the best geographic knowledge of Apollonius' era, the Danube split into two streams. One flowed north, while the other flowed into the Adriatic Sea. The Argonauts would follow that second stream. Then they could sail home.

Apsyrtus split his forces. Half headed for the exit from the Black Sea and the Hellespont. They would row into the Adriatic from its southern end and catch the Argonauts that way. The other half went with Apsyrtus, who figured out a shortcut to the Adriatic and would be waiting for Jason when he emerged.

The plan worked. Even though most of the Argonauts were great heroes, Apsyrtus had more than enough men to defeat them. There

CHAPTER 4

was no immediate battle. Aeëtes may have been more upset about the "kidnapping" of Medea than with losing the golden fleece. Apsyrtus suggested keeping Medea in a temple, until a local king could determine what would have to be done with her—whether she should stay with Jason or return home.

At first Jason seemed willing to negotiate, which upset Medea. She was afraid that Jason might agree to send her back in exchange for keeping the golden fleece. She had no desire to return home, as her father would probably kill her.

Medea suggested a secret meeting with Apsyrtus. He came alone, and he and Medea seemed to come to an agreement. However, the meeting wasn't quite as secret as Medea had told her brother it would be. Jason was in hiding nearby. He sprang out and struck down Apsyrtus.

Jason cut off Apsyrtus' hands and feet to make sure that his ghost couldn't pursue him. As a further part of this ritual, he slurped up and spit out his victim's blood three times.

The Argonauts tried to sail home, but they had committed a horrible crime by killing Apsyrtus. Zeus decided they had to be purified. The only one who could purify them was Circe (SIR-see), Medea's aunt. Her island home was on the other side of the Italian peninsula. Zeus sent a series of storms that blew them back to the north. The talking beam on *Argo* explained what they had to do.

They crossed the northern part of Italy and entered the Rhone River, in modern-day France. They took the wrong fork and headed north, where they surely would have met destruction. The Greeks were only dimly familiar with the region, but they knew it held a number of wild, warlike tribes. In fact, the Argonauts were only saved because Hera came down from Mount Olympus. She concealed them in mist so that their new enemies couldn't see them. Soon they turned around.

Now pointed in the right direction, they made their way down the coast of Italy to Circe's island. At first she welcomed them. Then she learned that they had murdered Apsyrtus. She purified them any-way and sent them on their way.

Then they arrived at Drepane (dree-PAA-nee), an island today known as Corfu. There they encountered the other group of soldiers from Colchis. There were even more of them than had been with Apsyrtus. These men demanded that Medea be returned to them. They left one loophole: If Medea were married to Jason, she could stay with him. Originally the couple had planned to wait until they returned to Iolchus to wed. Now they arranged a hasty marriage to satisfy the Colchians, who went back home.

Jason, Medea, and the Argonauts left Drepane, but a sudden storm came up. It blew them across the Mediterranean Sea to the desert of Libya, where they were stranded for a period of time. Finally they broke free and sailed for the island of Crete, where they had one more adventure. A giant bronze robot named Talus (TAY-lus) kept breaking off huge pieces of rock and throwing them at the *Argo*. The sailors couldn't go ashore to get food and water. Once again Medea came to the rescue. She gave Talus a withering look, which distracted him so much that he scraped his ankle—his one vulnera-ble spot—on a rock and collapsed into the sea. The Argonauts could complete their voyage.

"Happily you stepped upon the shores of Pagasae,"[2] Apollonius ends his poem, referring to the only port of Thessaly, the place where the expedition had also probably begun. But his readers and listen-ers knew there was more to the story, largely because of Euripides' play *Medea*, which had been written during the previous century.

Jason returned to Iolcus and delivered the golden fleece to Pelias, but he faced a major disappointment. Because he had been gone so long, most people believed he had died. Pelias felt that he could get rid of Aeson without fear of retribution. He forced Aeson to take poi-son. Aeson's wife, Polymele, had also been killed. Jason seethed with resentment, especially since he had kept his end of the bargain by bringing back the golden fleece. Now that Aeson was gone, Pelias

Medea (on the left) "shows" Pelias (on the right) that an old ram can be cut up and turned into a young lamb. Pelias fell for the trick, which cost him his life.

didn't show any signs that he was willing to give up being king.

Typically, it was Medea who thought of a solution. She went to Pelias and his daughters and explained that the goddess Artemis wanted her to do a favor for Pelias by making him young again. That way, he could continue to rule even longer.

Pelias wasn't convinced. Medea, who had used her magic to appear as an old woman, suddenly resumed her normal youthful appearance. "Such is the power of Artemis!" she cried.[3] To seal the deal, she killed an old ram. She cut it into many small pieces, threw them into a kettle, and let the kettle simmer for several hours over an open fire. When she took off the top, a little lamb sprang out and began romping around.

Pelias didn't need any further convincing. He told his daughters to kill him when he went to sleep that night, fully believing that he would awaken as a younger man. His daughters obeyed him. To their dismay, Pelias didn't come back to life.

Medea shrugged. She said she must have made a mistake. Actually she had fooled the daughters by using one of her magic spells to create the lamb. The old ram had really died.[4]

The residents of Iolcus were not amused. They forced Jason and Medea to leave. No one knows if they took the golden fleece with them. It seems to have disappeared after they gave it to King Pelias.

Circe

Medea and Circe (SIR-see) are two of the most notable witches in Greek myths. Unlike witches in later societies (who are usually hideously deformed), both women were very beautiful. Circe's father was Helios, the sun god, so she is a goddess herself. She lived on the island of Aeaea (ee-EE-uh), which is off the western coast of Italy.

She plays a prominent role in the *Odyssey*. Odysseus and his men land on Aeaea. He sends more than twenty of them ahead to explore the island while he remains behind to guard the ship.

From a distance, the men hear Circe singing sweetly. The songs attract them and they go closer. She greets them, surrounded by lions and wolves that seem surprisingly tame. In reality, they are the spirits of sailors she has transformed through her magic. She gives Odysseus' men a drink she says will refresh them, but it is actually a potion that turns them into pigs. She herds them into a pen and throws pig food at them.

Nineteenth-century artist John William Waterhouse shows Circe offering Odysseus a cup containing the same potion that has already turned his men into pigs. Odysseus overcomes her magic and obtains the release of his men.

One of the men has held back. From a hiding place, he sees what happens. He tells Odysseus, who decides to confront Circe. With the help of a potion given to him by the god Hermes, Odysseus isn't overcome by Circe's magic. When she taps him with her magic wand, nothing happens. Instead, he takes his sword and threatens her. He orders her to release all his men from their bondage as swine. She agrees and they become taller and better-looking than they were before.

Odysseus and his men spend a year on Aeaea. Circe gives him advice about the next stages of his journey. The crucial stage is his descent into the Underworld, where he will learn how to appease Poseidon so that he can finally get home.

Corinth, where Jason and Medea settled after returning from securing the golden fleece, was one of the most important cities of ancient Greece. It became very prosperous because of its extensive trade. It featured prominently in the early days of Christianity. The apostle Paul wrote two letters to its inhabitants; the letters survive as two books of the Bible's New Testament.

JASON

CHAPTER 5

Medea's Revenge

Jason and Medea settled in the city of Corinth, where they had two sons and seemed destined to have a happy life together. That situation changed when Jason got tired of Medea and wanted to marry Glauce (GLAW-see). She was the daughter of Creon (KREE-on), the king of Corinth. It would be a good marriage—for Jason. He was ambitious, and marrying the king's daughter would place him in line to become king when Creon died.

In Euripides' play, Medea bares her soul when she hears that Jason wants to leave her:

> On me this thing has fallen so unexpectedly,
> It has broken my heart. I am finished. I let go
> All my life's joy. My friends, I only want to die.
>   It was everything to me to think well of one man,
> and he, my own husband, has turned out wholly vile.
> Of all things which are living and can form a judgment
> We women are the most unfortunate creatures.[1]

She points out that women are second-class citizens, even though they have to undergo the intense pain of childbirth:

> A man, when he's tired of the company in his home
> Goes out of the house and puts an end to his boredom
> And turns to a friend or companion of his own age.
> But we are forced to keep our eyes on one alone.
> What they say of us is that we have a peaceful time
> Living at home, while they do the fighting in war.

Still holding the sword she used to kill her sons, Medea boards a wagon drawn by dragons and flees to Athens. The city's ruler, King Aegeus, welcomed her.

How wrong they are! I would very much rather stand
Three times in the front of battle than bear one child.[2]

She admits that women have to endure their status largely in silence. They can't complain. If they do, they may be beaten, cast aside, or even killed. For the most part, women in ancient Greece were afraid to speak out or take action against anything—but love was the one area in which they wouldn't stand aside.

In other ways a woman
Is full of fear, defenseless, dreads the sight of cold steel;
But when once she is wronged in the matter of love,
No other soul can hold so many thoughts of blood.[3]

Creon soon became aware of the danger that her unhappiness presented. After all, she was a witch. She could cast spells and work dark magic against his family. He ordered her to leave the city.

Now Medea was really desperate. It was bad enough that she was a foreigner. Now she would have the additional burden of two fatherless children, because Jason wouldn't want to keep the sons he'd had with Medea. He would want to start a new family with Glauce. It would be hard for Medea to find a home.

At this point, she began the plot that included murdering her sons. She was thorough in her planning. First she sent Glauce a poisoned robe that killed both her and her father. After killing her own sons, she fled in a dragon-drawn wagon from Corinth to Athens. She found shelter with King Aegeus, had a son named Medus with him, and eventually returned home to Colchis with this son. Medus killed Aeëtes and became king.

Later Medus expanded the kingdom to the east, where it became a vast empire. His descendants were called Medes; they were also known as Persians. Under that name, they became the great enemies of the Greeks during the last part of the sixth century and the start of the fifth century BCE. Because of the hostility between the two sides, the Greeks had good reason to claim that their foes owed their origins to a witch. In two famous battles, Marathon (490 BCE) and Salamis (480 BCE), the Greeks

Creon, the king of Corinth, holds his head in horror as his daughter Glauce rushes to a nearby fountain to put out the flames of the cloak that Medea sent her. The water couldn't quench the fire, which quickly spread and also consumed Creon. Some sources say the robe was poisoned.

defeated invading Persian armies. Those victories allowed them to establish their own society, which marked the beginning of democracy, or rule by the people. Before that, people were under the control of a king or of a few rulers.

Jason never recovered from the shock of Medea's crime. He spent several years wandering through Greece, alone and friendless. Then one day he found his old ship, beached and falling apart. He sat down next to it. The prow fell on him, killing him instantly. It was a humiliating end for a supposedly great hero.

Argo had a better fate. "The gods raised the ship to the sky and made it into a constellation,"[4] explain Grant and Hazel. Hercules, on the other hand, was welcomed into Mount Olympus, where he became a minor god.

In fact, Apollonius tells us, when the men first assembled, Jason urged them to

> Choose the best
> Man among you as leader, to look after all details,
> To settle quarrels, make agreements when we're in
>   foreign parts.[5]

To what must have been Jason's surprise, everyone chose Hercules to be the leader. He was the strongest and the best known among them. But Hercules declined. He said that the honor should go to the man who had organized the expedition, even though he was perhaps not the best qualified.

That isn't to say that Jason wasn't brave. His story is the first description of a long journey. At that time, water was the only real highway to travel great distances. Even then, no one traveled at night. The hours of darkness were occupied by monsters and demons. To go beyond Greece was an immense adventure, and Jason's journey was truly a voyage into the unknown. It required a great deal of courage.

Even so, Apollonius' story contains several departures from the heroic tradition. For one thing, Jason isn't quite as heroic as Hercules, Odysseus, Theseus, and other mythological figures. For them, it would have been unthinkable to allow a woman to take the lead—yet that is exactly what Jason repeatedly allows Medea to do.

When Jason first learns of the four-fold task that Aeëtes has given him, he seems to be depressed:

Jason, eyes fixed on the ground before him,
Sat there speechless, unmoving, at a loss in this crisis.
Long he considered the problem, tried every angle, yet
    dared not
Boldly take up the challenge, so huge a task it seemed.[6]

While he agrees to undertake the task, there's little question that he's clueless as to how he's going to go about doing it. It seems almost certain that he will perish. Yet he must do something, or Aeëtes will not give him the golden fleece. It would be too humiliating to return to Iolchus without it.

He only succeeds and stays alive because Medea falls in love with him and helps him. As he makes his final preparations, "Jason sprinkled himself with the lotion, and force coursed through him."[7]

Another time Medea helps him is when they enter the grove where the golden fleece is kept. She does all the heavy lifting:

Now as [the serpent] writhed
Medea forced it down, holding it with her eyes,
In sweet tones calling on Sleep . . .
Jason followed behind her in terror.[8]

A true hero isn't supposed to feel terror. The hero Hercules, for example, wouldn't have even needed Medea. He simply would have killed the dragon as he killed so many other monsters. And he wouldn't have required any encouragement to grab the golden fleece as Jason apparently does a little later, when the monster is safely asleep:

> Jason, at the girl's urging, reached into the oak tree
> And brought down the golden fleece.[9]

None of the other great Greek heroes would have allowed themselves to be led by a woman in this way.

Even though she is a foreigner, in a way Medea represents all the women of the city of Athens, the most famous city of ancient Greece. She has almost no rights except as the wife of Jason. Professor Barry Powell comments, "Euripides' *Medea* is the Athenian husband's worst nightmare come true, a ruthless woman who cannot control her violent emotions and her jealousy, who kills even her own children to settle a domestic dispute."[10]

The golden age of heroes seemed to be over. When Homer wrote his epic poetry several centuries earlier, Greek society was just starting to form. The Greeks needed to be reminded of their heroic past.

By Apollonius' time, conditions were different. Most Greeks lived in centralized city-states. People had obligations to each other. They needed to be reminded of what had gone before, but the rule of law had replaced the rule of strong men.

It is indeed a horrible thing that Medea does, but Jason is the one who sets these events in motion when he tries to abandon her and further his own career by marrying a princess. The family probably would have been just fine if Jason hadn't betrayed Medea.

Jason doesn't realize his own guilt. He insists that everything that happened is Medea's fault, rather than his own. Perhaps Euripides is saying that it is important for people to take responsibility for their own actions. If they don't, the consequences can be devastating.

Euripides

Euripides was the third of three famous playwrights who lived and thrived in ancient Athens. The first two were Aeschylus (525–456 BCE) and Sophocles (496–406 BCE).

According to legend, Euripides was born on September 23, 480 BCE. It was the same day as the Greek victory over the Persians at the Battle of Salamis. The battle played a major role in freeing the Greeks from the threat of Persian domination. What became known as the "Golden Age of Greece" immediately followed. This Golden Age became famous for political advances, outstanding architecture, and plays that are still performed today.

Repudiated by Jason, Medea takes her revenge by killing the two children she has borne to him; the subject is taken from Euripides' tragedy *Medea*.

Scholars believe that Euripides came from a wealthy family. He would have received a first-rate education and been exposed to the ideas of many leading thinkers of the era. There is also evidence that he was an outstanding athlete and a painter.

He was married twice and had at least three children. No one knows when he began writing plays. At that time, there was an annual playwriting contest in Athens. He entered for the first time in 455 BCE and placed third. It took fourteen more years for him to win first prize. He won four more times during the course of his career, during which he wrote nearly 100 plays. Only eighteen have survived over the centuries.

He is especially famous for depicting strong women in his plays. He might also be called more realistic than either Aeschylus or Sophocles because he shows how his characters think and feel. Powell points out that the famous Greek philosopher Aristotle "remarked that Sophocles showed men as they ought to be, but Euripides showed them as they really are."[11]

Another legend surrounds Euripides' death in 406 BCE. It is said that he had the misfortune to encounter a pack of rabid dogs. They attacked him and mauled him so severely, he died a few days later.

Chapter 1. A Monstrous Crime

1. Euripides, Euripides 1, The Complete Greek Tragedies, The Medea, translated by Rex Warner (New York: Washington Square Press, 1968), p. 110.

2. Ibid., pp. 112–113.

3. Ibid., p. 111.

4. Ibid., p. 112.

5. Ibid.

6. Tim Severin, *The Jason Voyage* (New York: Simon and Schuster, 1985), p. 21.

7. Michael Wood, *In Search of Myths and Heroes* (Berkeley: University of California Press, 2005), p. 91.

8. Homer, *The Odyssey*, translated by Robert Fagles (New York: Penguin Books, 1996), p. 273.

9. Robert Graves, *The Greek Myths* (New York: Penguin Books, 1992), p. 577.

Chapter 2. The Argo Sets Out

1. Mark P.O. Morford and Robert J. Lenardon, *Classical Mythology,* Fifth Edition (White Plains, New York: Longman Publishers, 1995), p. 472.

2. Ibid., p. 475.

3. Tim Severin, *The Jason Voyage* (New York: Simon and Schuster, 1985), p. 133.

4. Ibid., p. 132.

5. Apollonius of Rhodes, *The Argonautika: The Story of Jason and the Quest for the Golden Fleece*, translated by Peter Green (Berkeley: University of California Press, 1997), p. 94.

Chapter 3. The Golden Fleece

1. Michael Wood, *In Search of Myths and Heroes* (Berkeley: University of California Press, 2005), p. 105.

2. Tim Severin, *The Jason Voyage* (New York: Simon and Schuster, 1985), p. 204.

3. Apollonius of Rhodes, *The Argonautika: The Story of Jason and the Quest for the Golden Fleece*, translated by Peter Green (Berkeley: University of California Press, 1997), p. 147.

4. Michael Grant and John Hazel, *Who's Who in Classical Mythology* (New York: Routledge, 1999), p. 25.

5. Amazons in Greek Mythology http://www.geocities.com/hollywood/lot/5775/amazons.html

Chapter 4. Homeward Bound

1. Michael Wood, *In Search of Myths and Heroes* (Berkeley: University of California Press, 2005), pp. 134–135.

2. Apollonius of Rhodes, *The Argonautika: The Story of Jason and the Quest for the Golden Fleece*, translated by Peter Green (Berkeley: University of California Press, 1997), p. 198.

3. Robert Graves, *The Greek Myths* (New York: Penguin Books, 1992), p. 613.

4. Ibid., pp. 613–614.

Chapter 5. Medea's Revenge

1. Euripides, *Euripides 1, The Complete Greek Tragedies, The Medea,*

CHAPTER NOTES

translated by Rex Warner (New York: Washington Square Press, 1968), p. 71.

2. Ibid., p. 72.

3. Ibid.

4. Michael Grant and John Hazel, *Who's Who in Classical Mythology* (New York: Routledge, 1999), p. 47.

5. Apollonius of Rhodes, *The Argonautika: The Story of Jason and the Quest for the Golden Fleece*,

translated by Peter Green (Berkeley: University of California Press, 1997), p. 52.

6. Ibid., p. 124.

7. Ibid., p. 146.

8. Ibid., p. 155.

9. Ibid.

10. Barry Powell, *Classical Myth* (Upper Saddle River, New Jersey: Pearson Educational, 2004), p. 502.

11. Ibid., p. 68.

FURTHER READING

Books

Brooks, Felicity. *Jason and the Argonauts*. London: Usborne Books, 2005.

Catran, Ken. *Voyage with Jason*. Melbourne, Australia: Lothian Books, 2000.

Evslin, Bernard. *Jason and the Argonauts*. New York: William Morrow, 1986.

Whiting, Jim. *Hercules*. Hockessin, Delaware: Mitchell Lane Publishers, 2007.

Yolen, Jane, and Robert J. Harris. *Jason and the Gorgon's Blood*. New York: HarperCollins, 2004.

Zarabouka, Sofia. *Jason and the Golden Fleece: The Most Adventurous and Exciting Expedition of All the Ages*. Los Angeles: Getty Publications Trust, 2004.

Works Consulted

Apollonius of Rhodes. *The Argonautika: The Story of Jason and the Quest for the Golden Fleece*. Translated by Peter Green. Berkeley: University of California Press, 1997.

Beye, Charles Rowan. *Ancient Epic Poetry: Homer, Apollonius, Virgil*. Ithaca, New York: Cornell University Press, 1993.

FURTHER READING

Cahill, Thomas. *Sailing the Wine-Dark Sea: Why the Greeks Matter*. New York: Doubleday, 2003.

Euripides. *Euripides 1, The Complete Greek Tragedies. The Medea*. Translated by Rex Warner. New York: Washington Square Press, 1968.

Grant, Michael, and John Hazel. *Who's Who in Classical Mythology*. New York: Routledge, 1999.

Graves, Robert. *The Greek Myths*. New York: Penguin Books, 1992.

Hamilton, Edith. *Mythology*. New York: Warner Books, 1999.

Homer. *The Odyssey*. Translated by Robert Fagles. New York: Penguin Books, 1996.

Kerényi, C. *Heroes of the Greeks*. Translated by Professor H. J. Rose. London: Thames and Hudson, 1959.

Lefkowitz, Mary. *Greek Gods, Human Lives: What We Can Learn from Myths*. New Haven, Connecticut: Yale University Press, 2003.

Morford, Mark P.O., and Robert J. Lenardon. *Classical Mythology*. Fifth Edition. White Plains, New York: Longman Publishers, 1995.

Powell, Barry P. *Classical Myth*. Upper Saddle River, New Jersey: Pearson Educational, 2004.

Severin, Tim. *The Jason Voyage*. New York: Simon and Schuster, 1985.

Wood, Michael. *In Search of Myths and Heroes*. Berkeley: University of California Press, 2005.

On the Internet

Jason, the Argonauts and the Golden Fleece. http://www.mythweb.com/heroes/jason/index.html.

Jason and the Argonauts. http://www.greece.org/poseidon/work/argonautika/argo.html.

Jason and the Argonauts. http://www.pccc.cc.nj.us/asrc/readwrit/jason.html.

Stewart, Michael. "Kirke," *Greek Mythology: From the Iliad to the Fall of the Last Tyrant*. http://messagenet.com/myths/bios/circe.html.

Amazons in Greek Mythology. http://www.geocities.com/hollywood/lot/5775/amazons.html.

archaeologist (ar-kee-AH-luh-jist)—A person who scientifically studies objects from a past culture in order to better understand it.

centaur (SEN-tar)—A mythical creature that has the body of a horse and the head and torso of a man.

city-state—A small state or nation consisting of a city and the surrounding territory.

cyclops (SY-klops)—A member of the race of giants who had one huge eye in the center of their forehead.

epic poem (EH-pik POH-um)—A very long poem that describes the adventures of a real or imaginary hero.

fleece—The coat of wool that covers the skin of an animal such as a sheep.

immortal (ih-MOR-tul)—Never dying.

monotony (muh-NAH-tuh-nee)—Boredom; doing the same thing over and over.

nymph (NIMF)—A minor nature goddess.

oracle (OR-uh-kul)—A person through which hidden meanings or concealed knowledge are revealed; also, the shrine in which such a person may be consulted.

prophecy (PRAH-feh-see)—Prediction about the future.

prow—The front of a ship.

white caps—Waves that break into white foam at their tops.

INDEX